The Parrot and the Fig Tree

The Parrot and the Fig Tree

A Jataka Tale

Illustrated by Michael Harman

DHARMA PUBLISHING

First published 1990

Second edition 2009, augmented with guidance
for parents and teachers

Printed on acid-free paper

Printed in the United States of America by Dharma Press
35788 Hauser Bridge Road, Cazadero, California 95421

9   8   7   6   5   4   3

Library of Congress Cataloging-in-Publication Data

The Parrot and the Fig Tree

(Jataka Tales Series)
Summary: A parrot who dwells happily in a fig tree is tested for his loyalty
to the tree by Shakra, the king of gods.

Jataka stories, English. [1. Jataka stories]
I. Harman, Michael, ill. II. Series
BQ1462.E5 H37 1986   294.3'823   86-19769

ISBN 978-0-89800-430-4

Dedicated to children everywhere

Once upon a time in the far-off land of India, a flock of brightly colored parrots lived in a grove of fig trees on the banks of the river Ganges. Large green leaves shaded them from the sun. All day the birds flew through the branches, feeding on the sweet, juicy fruit that hung from the trees like deep blue garlands.

Among them was a magnificent parrot. This great bird lived happily in the same tree year after year, eating one fruit at a time. The tree gave him shelter and food in abundance and the parrot took pleasure in listening to the breeze playing with the leaves in his home under the tree's canopy. The magnificent parrot was grateful to his friend the fig tree and they lived together in harmony.

Most other parrots scurried from tree to tree, anxiously searching for the most perfect fruit, taking bites from only the ripest parts and discarding seeds, rinds and everything else they did not want. Excited and chattering, they did not notice how they were breaking small branches, spoiling the fruit and scattering the rinds and seeds everywhere.

Each year, as winter approached and the fruit began to drop on the ground or wither on the branches, the birds flew away. Only the magnificent parrot felt no need to leave his tree. When there were no more figs, he ate left-over rinds and seeds on the ground, or pieces of bark and leaves. Summer, fall, winter, and spring the parrot stayed near his friend the fig tree, growing happier and happier each passing season.

One day, his happiness became so complete that the parrot radiated waves of love and joy. The powerful waves reached the palace of Shakra, king of heavenly beings. Shakra's entire palace began to tremble; the carpets billowed, the candles flickered and the silk curtains loosened from their sashes.

Shakra wondered what could have caused
such a disturbance. He opened his magical eye
and from the heavens he looked down upon the
land of India. There he saw the magnificent parrot
perched in his fig tree, in perfect balance. Shakra
marveled at the parrot's contentment and decided
to test the bird's devotion.

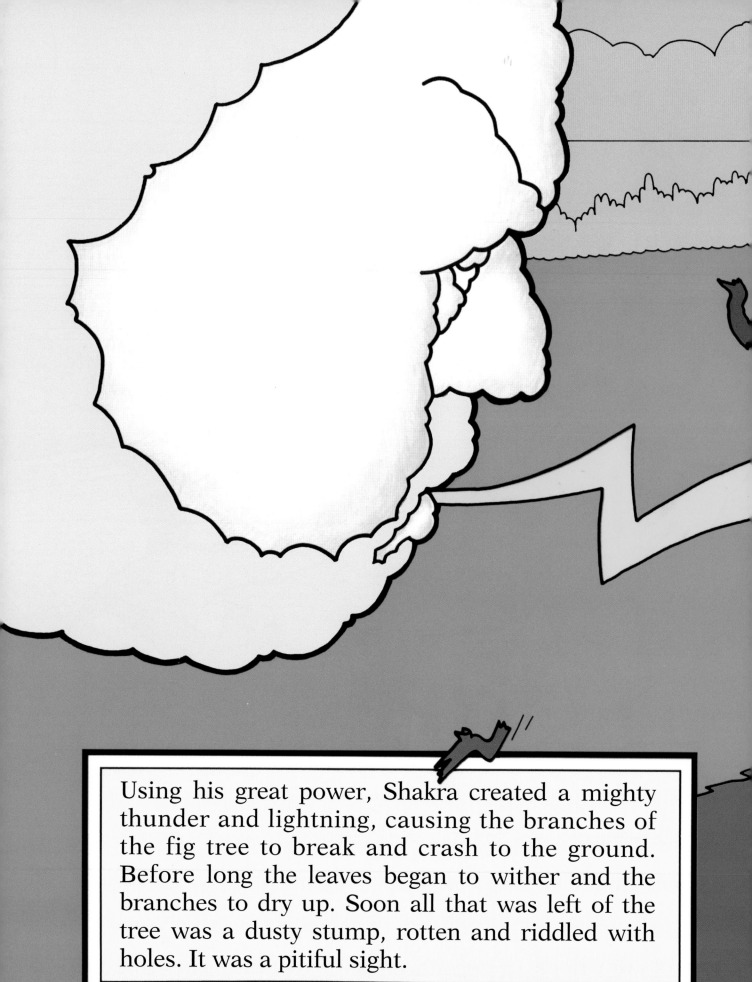

Using his great power, Shakra created a mighty thunder and lightning, causing the branches of the fig tree to break and crash to the ground. Before long the leaves began to wither and the branches to dry up. Soon all that was left of the tree was a dusty stump, rotten and riddled with holes. It was a pitiful sight.

Still the magnificent parrot did not leave the old tree. He perched on top of the stump and seemed satisfied with whatever he could find, eating the dust that the wind blew through the tree's holes and drinking water from the nearby river. When Shakra saw that the parrot was as content as before, even without a safe home and tasty food, the king of gods said to himself, "This is indeed an unusual parrot. I would like to hear him explain why he does not move to a healthier tree."

Shakra changed himself into a royal goose with broad graceful wings and flew to the forest where the magnificent parrot lived. He called out to the parrot and said, "I know that parrots crave a fruit-filled tree. But when there is no fruit left, most birds fly away. Why do you, all alone, cling to this tree that will never bloom again? Make haste and leave today!"

The magnificent parrot listened to the royal goose's words without uttering a sound. As he sat motionless, his feathers shone in the sunlight.

Shakra spoke again,
"This old stump of a tree will not protect you from the winter's cold and wind, nor feed you when you are hungry. Do you not fear for your life? Fly away, my friend, please fly away quickly! Join the flocks that are feasting on fresh ripe fruit in southern lands!"

At last the magnificent parrot opened his bill and spoke, "Since ancient times, friends have been content to support each other through good times and bad. They know how to be faithful, and never forget to be good to one another. So I too wish to stand by this tree that has given me shelter and food for so many years. Yes, I want to live, but I will not part from my old friend in distress, even if he can no longer help me."

Delighted with the parrot's loyalty and appreciation for his friend the fig tree, Shakra praised him, saying, "I know your friendship and love are true. Those who are wise honor their friends just as you do. For your faithfulness I will grant you a wish. You may wish for anything you like. Tell me, what would make your kind heart happiest?"

Without a moment's hesitation the magnificent parrot answered, "O greatest of geese, if you would give me what I wish most, please make my dear friend, the fig tree, come back to life again. This good tree has never harmed anyone. Please, let this tree grow new branches and leaves, gather fresh water from its roots, and bear healthy fruit."

Shakra changed back into his godly form. Seated upon his magic carpet, he swooped down to the river, took up water and splashed it on the dying tree. Instantly the tree sprang into life and as the magnificent parrot watched, he saw the trunk grow strong and new branches begin to sprout. Soon figs sweet as honey hung down from all its branches until the tree gleamed like a mountain of deep blue jewels.

Then Shakra said to the magnificent parrot, "See, my friend, here before you stands a strong tree, a fitting home for a loyal bird such as you."

Filled with joy and gratitude, the magnificent parrot thanked Shakra, king of heavenly beings, saying, "May you and all those you love be blessed with great joy and good fortune, just as I am blessed seeing my dear friend and companion come back to life." Then the magnificent parrot snuggled into his favorite niche in the top of the tree.

With this, Shakra left the parrot and the fig tree. He returned to his palace in the sky, knowing that the two friends would live out the rest of their days together in happiness and peace.

My page

Colored by _____

The Jataka Tales nurture in readers young and old an appreciation for values shared by all the world's great spiritual traditions. Read aloud, performed and studied for centuries, they communicate universal values such kindness, forgiveness, compassion, humility, courage, honesty and patience. You can bring this story alive through the suggestions on these pages. Actively engaging with the stories creates a bridge to the children in your life and opens a dialogue about what brings joy, stability and caring.

The Parrot And The Fig Tree

A magnificent parrot lives happily in a luscious fig tree, surrounded by brightly colored companions. When summer is over, the other parrots fly away in search of more abundant places to feast on ripe fruit. Instead of following the flock, our parrot remains loyal to his companion the fig tree. When his devotion is put to a test by the king of the gods, the parrot remains a steadfast friend to the fig tree and thus demonstrates the value of true friendship.

Key Values
Loyalty
Friendship
Wise use of natural resources

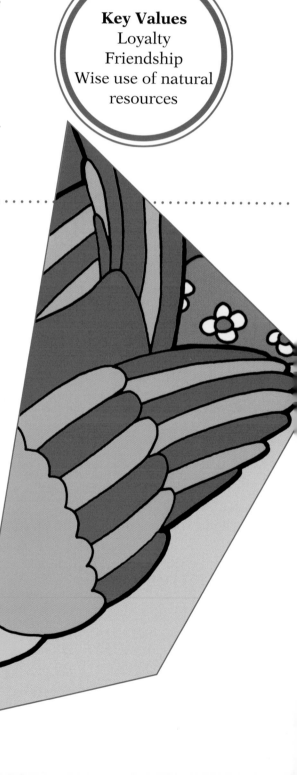

Bringing the story to life

Engage the children by asking at the turning of a page: "What do you think will happen next?"

Asking the children questions about the events and values in the story will deepen their understanding and enrich their vocabulary. For example:

• In what way is the magnificent parrot unusual?
• Why are trees important to animals? And to us?
• If you were a tree, what would your message be?
• Why does Shakra use water to revive the tree?
• Do you have a good friend like the parrot?

Discussion topics and questions can be modified depending on the age of your child.

Learning through play

Children love to try out new ideas and use all five senses to make discoveries. You can encourage their creativity and help them play with ideas that the narrative brings up:

- Have the children color in or draw a scene or character that intrigues them. Then invite them to talk about what it means to them, exploring the key values.
- Make masks for all the characters.
- Paint the masks and decorate them.
- Let each child choose a character to impersonate. Imitate the voices, and bring the qualities of the parrot, the royal goose and Shakra to life. Then switch roles.
- Display the key values somewhere visible and refer to them regularly.
- Have the children re-tell you the story. Ask them why the characters act the way they do.

Active reading

- Even before children can read, they enjoy storybooks and love growing familiar with the characters and drawings. You can show them the pictures in this book and tell the story in your own words.
- You can prepare by reading the book first yourself. By reading the book to the children a few times and helping them to recognize words, you encourage them to build vocabulary.
- Children love to hear the same story over and over, with different and maybe exaggerated voices for each character.
- Intgrate the wisdom of the story into everyday life. When tempers flare or patience is called for, remind the child of the parrot's wisdom, or other qualities.
- Talk about the story while you and the children are engaged in daily activities like washing the dishes or driving to school.

Glossary

India: The source of many spiritual traditions and the background of most of the Jatakas (accounts of the Buddha's previous lives). People seeking wisdom have always viewed India's forests and jungles as favorable places for solitary retreats. The Buddha taught the Jatakas to clarify the workings of karma, the relationship between actions and results.

River Ganges: Winding 1,500 miles across northern India, the river is revered as a goddess and plays a role in many myths.

Devotion: feelings of love for someone or something.

Loyalty: faithfulness to a person or a cause.

Shakra: also known as Indra, is the king of gods; the Indian equivalent of Zeus or Jupiter.

The Jataka Tales are folk tales that were transmitted orally, memorized and passed from generation to generation for hundreds of years. We are grateful for the opportunity to offer them to you. May they inspire fresh insight into the dynamics of human relationships and may understanding grow with each reading.

The Jataka Tales are for children aged three to eight

JATAKA TALES SERIES

The Best of Friends

Courageous Captain

The Fish King's Power of Truth

Golden Foot

Great Gift and the
   Wish-Fulfilling Gem

Heart of Gold

The Hunter and the Quail

The Jewel of Friendship

The King Who
   Understood Animals

The Magic of Patience

The Monkey King

The Monster of Lotus Lake

The Parrot and the Fig Tree

Pieces of Gold

The Power of a Promise

A Precious Life

The Princess Who
   Overcame Evil

The Proud Peacock

The Rabbit in the Moon

The Rabbit Who Overcame Fear

The Spade Sage

Three Wise Birds

The Value of Friends

Wisdom of the Golden Goose

A Wise Ape Teaches Kindness